SHAPESHIFTING FOR BEGINNERS

T0351241

ALSO BY EMMA SIMON

PAMPHLETS

The Odds (Smith|Doorstop, 2020)

Dragonish (The Emma Press, 2017)

EMMA SIMON

Shapeshifting for Beginners

SALT

SHEFFIELD

PUBLISHED BY SALT PUBLISHING 2023

2 4 6 8 10 9 7 5 3 1

First published in Great Britain in 2023 by
Salt Publishing Ltd
18 Churchill Road, Sheffield, S10 1FG United Kingdom
www.saltpublishing.com

Salt Publishing Limited Reg. No. 5293401

A CIP catalogue record for this book is available from the British Library

ISBN 978 1 78463 285 4 (Paperback edition)

Typeset in Sabon by Salt Publishing

Printed and bound in Great Britain by Clays Ltd, Elcograf S.p.A

To my family, with love

'The human body is precisely our capacity for metamorphosis. The body is itself a kind of place – not a solid object but a terrain through which things pass. [. . .] Sometimes the world's textures move across this threshold unchanged. Sometimes they are transformed by the passage. And sometimes they reshape the doorway itself.'

DAVID ABRAM, *Becoming Animal*

'In the end we'll all become stories.'

MARGARET ATWOOD, *Moral Disorder & Other Stories*

Contents

Shapeshifting for Beginners

A Mermaid's Complaint

I told the therapist, these aren't my legs.
Mine shouldn't be so solid. I never thought
they'd root me to the ground like trunks.
A man described them as a sturdy set of pins
and he was right: like upturned skittles,
waiting to be bowled over. Look at this spread
of knees, how my thighs stick together
on a hot bus, skirts ride and wrinkle,
trousers cling. These bloody legs are mutinous.
Sometimes I try to punish them, make them run.
To pay me back they trudge with all their weight
round supermarket aisles, complain and ache
up stairs. Lowered in a bath they sink,
all stubbled shins and razor rash. I cover up
their shame with foamy bubbles. Some nights
I dream of knives filleting a bream or bass,
pressing the sharp point beneath the skin
to lift away the excess meat, leaving just
a clean curve of bone. The kind of legs
ballerinas pirouette on, sequins on their tutus
glinting in the light, hard as silver fish scales.

The Derry Street Trials

If she crooks a knowing smile your way
to draw out thoughts that itch within,
then she's a witch.

Scrutinise her dress. If it's raggedy,
hem unstitched or wanton split too high,
then she's a witch.

If you can see the bones of her,
a jut of question marks, a lack of marrow,
then she's a skinny witch.

They are the worst. Though many shape-shift,
disguise their witchy forms
in outsize black and formless grey,

roll malicious intent, year after year,
in thick fat, like the truffling pigs
they want to turn you into.

If you see such figures in the tented dark,
laughing at the night while gathering its riches,
beware. They're all likely witches.

Mark her hair; if there are silver streaks
– known as devil's moonshine – it's a sure sign
she's an accomplished witch.

If she has no children. Or too many.
Leaves them a-bed while she slips out
to conjure coins from the beamy air,

or stays at home, bricked behind her walls
without a man to breathe life in her fire,
then she's a witch,

or as good as, by any rational reckoning.
Watch her by the water:
how she skirts the millpond.

Leverets

Hares sleep with their eyes open.
And I thought of that, strangely,
as she stood by the side of my bed
skin flushed, hair stuck to her forehead
as though she'd been running
through the night, now shivery
in thin pyjamas. Mummy wake up,
she said, the trees are coming.
The dreaming like the dead are heavy
to hold, carry into the antiseptic light
of a tiled bathroom. As I flannelled
her face, watched eyes start to focus,
I chided myself for that backward glance
into the hall, where the empty house
shifted the bones of itself in the darkness.
Just fever-dreams I said, she nodded,
and whispered in her daytime voice,
but the trees are waiting. Lifting her
back to bed I made a show of checking,
then closing wardrobe doors, the window,
to lock out the cold and creep of damp,
fingertip reach of wayward branches.
Placed a hand on the fluttering chest
of her sleeping sister, who remained
her fully female self, for now at least.

Living With Poltergeists

It will be temporary you say: the door banging
with the slam of a headache, again and again.

Evenings when fierce air settles on the landing,
passes like a cold front through each room.

Drawers half ransacked, lights left on, a chaos
of shoes. It could be worse. Your sister spoke

of a blazer shredded, scissors dancing in the light.
Spirits of long-dead saints sometimes visit,

their shadows on the stairs, thin as painted frescoes.
We're fearful of stigmata, the whispered tales

of blood-caked tissues scrunched up in the bin.
We know that sleeplessness is not an absolute,

nights can be worried wider by degrees.
One friend saw a porcelain statue break

into spontaneous tears. She lay awake in bed,
scared the house would wash away on them.

The worst of it: we recognise this pent-up power,
remember when we could walk through walls

and stagger out the other side, slip out of our skin
like quicksilver eels. Our confidence in miracles,

that things would just get better. All those little changelings
now fixed in place, rigid as our own dead mothers.

What would they tell us now we wonder,
as we gather round the table, pour the coffee,

confess to each other just how bad it's got.
Watch steam rise from the cups like prayer.

Escaped Balloons

The closest thing to ghosts
you'll see these days:

unearthed, unribboned,
drifting in a summer sky.

A silver zero catching the sun,
last trace of one hell of a party,

the drinks all drunk, and no more
birthdays counted now from here.

A pierced heart snagged in branches
unable to float on, pass through.

The rainbow dazzle of a Peppa Pig
that's slipped a chubby fist

and climbed up into silence.
No-one knows for sure how high

they go, what happens as they rise
into colder stratospheres,

disappear from view. Do they burst
into clouds of foil confetti,

dissolve as glints in rain? Blink
and all you'll see are sunspots

dancing in the blue,
those visual disturbances

you sometimes get from staring
into empty space too long.

Bird

I sing in the key of bittern, laugh the hollow bones
of hungry pelican. Inside my brain I've locked away
the path of stars depicted in the almanacs of sparrow.
I throb with the green streak of wood pigeon,
a flush of robin at my throat. I have a cuckoo's nose
for half a chance, that magpie glint for trouble.
I am the single swallow of uncertain summer,
too late now for worms. I stand a ragtag cormorant
on the rock with salt-dried wings, the jenny wren
who picks at crumbs from wedding cakes.
I ruffle with flamingo pink, curse ungainly knees.
Hen's teeth are not as uncommon as you think;
mine chatter with eggshell grit, while my heart,
that poor caged goose, grows fatter and fatter.

Dear bees –

I know it's a lot to bear,
these half-voiced mumblings and frets
among the budding lavender.
It's not as if you haven't got
your own troubles to worry about,
but here I go, trowel in hand,
making heavy work of the weeds.
I'm no longer sure if I'm digging up
dandelions or anemones.
Listen, the news isn't good today
but I guess you knew that,
bumbling stalk to stalk, garden to garden
to the frazzled hums
of one more disappointment.
Do we weigh down your wings
with all these confessions?
Secrets charging your cells like batteries,
gossipy snippets stuck to your legs
as you rise from the buddleia.
We unburden ourselves to an afternoon sky,
our little striped consciences.
Look at them fly. Through the fence I saw
a woman next door kneel down by the border,
the sound of her prayers
drowned out by the continual loops
of the lawn sprinkler.

Quantum Theory of Moss

The world's slowest moving magic carpet,
knitting the years across the sodden ground.
A velvet pole star, frizzled, fallen, rootbound.
The green man's goatee, overgrown and matted.
A secret diary of the damp, the dark,
its tangled thoughts an urgent scribbled mess.
A concrete car-park's favourite summer dress,
flock wallpaper adorning knotty bark.
Dishevelled grass. A mop to blot the dew.
Entwined necklaces strung with emerald beads,
a glass of chartreuse drunk amid the weeds,
spring-soft mattress and morning after hairdo.
The songs of home, holding stones in place.
Waves of reflected leaf-light, moving at snail's pace.

Mushrooms

They take their vow of silence seriously.
　　Absorb the crunch of leaf litter, the creak
of rotting trunks into their hooded caps.

All plants know quietness, but mushrooms feed
　　on it. They suck all calm, all sense of ease
from autumn evenings, mulch it to monkish hush.

They practice stillness: gills unfluttered
　　by the breeze. No silky petal swish.
Their very noiselessness seems held in check

deliberately. Mouths buttoned up. Their thoughts
　　sprout in the darkness, take pale shapes
of mothwing whiteness, like shadows on a scan.

They know it's will not words which give prayer
　　power. Stood circled, smooth heads bowed
together, morph into things we cannot say.

Mammogram

You've learned to hug the machine.
Stood there, right breast viced
between the X-ray plates.

Your arm draped round its hulk,
head leaning in, as though to rest
on its plasticated shoulder.

Its grip tightens. Then lets you go.
The sort of gruff lover you might find
brooding in Victorian novels.

A rough touch, with little time
for niceties, whose stare unsettles
hidden vulnerabilities.

In this darkened room you share
strange intimacies. Clammy skin
pressed flat against cold metal.

You're conscious of your naked belly,
the way you scoop around its body,
the slight catch of your breath.

The nurse does not say much
glancing at your family history,
adjusts the placing of your elbow,

tells you to squeeze in closer.
You hold on tight, its solid bulk
the only stable thing to cling to.

Poem that is haunted by the ghost of my mother, singing, and a fleeting after-image of Emily Dickinson

Another one, if I'm honest. Sometimes I put my ear
to the page to make out the words –
but it's just that trapped fly buzzing of my brain.

I'll be writing a poem, about lemons or something,
trying to taste the zest by conjuring a tree,
an afternoon in Italy, lunch in the shade.

But the shadows won't play ball. They're whispering
between the pavement cracks. My fingernails
are worn to the quick trying to drag them out.

Sometimes I try to shake out ghosts from other books
stacked on my shelves. I know they're there,
that sense of someone watching from the margins.

I trace words across the page and feel the static.
The lines are scattered ashes now strangely magnetised,
like those iron filing experiments we did at school.

When you're dead why would you hang out
in some clock-stopped house or boxed-up attic,
combing cobwebs from your hair?

Luxuriate here instead, in all this white space,
enjoying the lemon spritz, swish of summer breeze
through plane trees, or whatever else this poem

or the next might be about. Come on,
don't tell me you can't hear her, now and again,
singing slightly out of tune.

Guide wanted

or perhaps not wanted, needed now.
I hear that sometimes works.

Someone with proven competencies
in dead ends and T-Junctions,
who knows how to untangle woods.

Experience of incoming weather fronts,
chess gambits, emoji-speak preferred.
Not necessarily some*one*. I'm open

to resumés from sparrow hawks
and ash trees, the wisdom of moss
summarised on a single-sheet CV.

Can you solve the riddle of an egg
in less than twenty words, wrap it up
in a story spooled from high-tensile yarn,

knit shadows into hoodies and disappear
in crowds? Please leave your application
at the end of a crazy paving trail

of crumbs/ pavement gum/ pine cones/
(delete as required). Successful candidates
will be waiting by the gatepost,

whistling some familiar tune, counting
the furthest ripples made from skimming stones.

The Gardeners

I want to be one of those women
with sturdy gloves
who knows how to pinch out,

or angle a knife for stem cuttings.
I want the simplicity
of growing them on in a glass of clear water.

I want to gather things in
by the armful, see my own fingerprints
whorled through the dirt.

I want to hoard seeds in brown envelopes,
slip Latin names under my tongue,
hang secateurs up on a peg

after deadheading frowsy pink roses.
I want to learn kitchen secrets
for warding off slugs.

I want to cultivate shade,
to know how they catch morning sunlight
inside a cold frame.

I want their easy optimism
that next spring there will be apple blossom,
their tree-like patience.

I want to weather like them,
faces turned to tomorrow,
to let my hair silver not grey in the rain.

My Life as a B-List Movie Star

You know what it's like, Monday mornings,
battling astro-zombies in a silver bikini,
primordial swampthings, robot killercats.

Is the ray gun fully charged, set to stun?
Can you outwit the brain-that-won't-die
while cleanly severing tentacles?

God, there is so much to do. Though by lunch
you're suckered in quicksand or luminous ooze
slimed by the man-sized slugs.

To be honest, this life isn't the highball glitz
I'd imagined. It's hard, running in heels
from lumbering bearsuits, screaming at shadows.

Some days a malevolent fog whispers its way
under locked doors, up the stairs. And you shrink
bit by bit, slip into the watery depths

of an olive-spiked glass. Tread water naked.
You can flash them your best fifty-foot smile,
Don, Dan or Sam or whoever else is manfully

making his way to the rescue. Eyes all the same,
bright pockets of sky, whose laser-like glares
fail to pierce the dark heart of your problems.

On the phone to your mother you ponder
alternate futures, madness ragging her voice
when she mentions secretarial courses, neat homes

hemmed in on all sides by white fences.
You dream of a world where warrior queens
can have nondescript breasts, less bouffant hair,

be beyond the forbidden. Is everyone freaked
by this spidery sense they picked the wrong part,
watching tarantulas crawl up the walls?

Someone else has the script where you star
in a dazzling life that feels solid and real.
You know what it's like, marooned on the palm

of a hand before it snaps shut, watching lights
flicker out on a plywood cutout of your hopes
that once soared like the Empire State Building.

The Alarms

You said you didn't hear that car alarm.
Slept through. It didn't call you
from the other side of sleep
back to this dark square of a room.

My waking self is quite alone
listening to the pain of a Honda Civic.
Insistent. Like an animal trapped
by the orange glare of street lights.

An anxious blare. Wallpaper noise.
Its pattern easy to ignore in daylight.
But now, with the wardrobe eating
its own shadows, hard to block out.

There are quiet gaps I could fall into,
where the alarm catches its breath,
and the night pulls a thick blanket
over its head. Pretends to settle down.

Until sound flares again. A lock
somewhere bust open. A headache
of hot stars pressed into my pillow,
the clocks in my bones all ringing.

Part of me can't hear the moon calling anymore

Isn't it always the same, within a crisis
another smaller crisis following its own orbit.
For years now I've been singing to her tunes
listening to the pluck of strings inside me,
a grate of pebbles raked back by the tide.
Moons are like gods, they're not restricted
to the night. She'd stalk me at odd times,
appearing in a shower, or as I stood
with nothing to protect me in a changing room.
More often though she'd slip between my legs
slick and tangled up in last night's sheets.
I've watched moonlight drip through windows,
puddling in splashes on the bathroom floor,
felt her fingers tightening their grip. But now
she pretends not to know me. Though I cursed
her stupid dance, this hunt, it's kind of lonely
watching her up there, peeling off one mask,
then slipping on another. I feel two empty holes
where her eyes should be. I am lost to time
where distances are measured out in years,
and all the little stars inside extinguished,
one by one, they're blinking out their lights.

Emily at 49
After Bagpuss

I feel a little loose myself these days
unpicked at the seams when I remember

all those doors now closed, alarms set
for the night. And sometimes when I'm feeling

like I sometimes do, I sag on the settee,
scroll through hours and hours of snow

on the CCTV, watching how nothing
moves now. I stand in front of shop displays

transfixed by all this stuff, as if reed infusers
willow pattern plates, a batik sarong

might be that misplaced sense of the marvellous
I've lost. I want the girl who's gone

who dreamed in candy-coloured stripes.
Please don't read too much into the cats.

They prowl the skirting boards at night,
chasing shadows, as though they hear

the ghost of Charlie Mouse still singing
how he will fix us up.

The Women At The Swimming Pool

What I wouldn't give to stand
at the deep-end edge and spring
from my body. Leave this flesh
squeezed in a purple one-piece,
and carve through the air as a dart.
Look at the woman beside me,
all bound-up potential, ready to dive,
fingertips stretched to open a hole
in the pool's surface, pull herself through.
It's true, those old myths: how we step
out of endless to-do lists and worries
leave them hung up on pegs
with our coats. See how she turns
like a glorious otter, all sunlight
and splash down the slow lane,
the swimmer beside her floating away
from those Slimming World sins,
light and lithe as an eel once again.
Sleek heads bob with the wisdom of seals.
Wet footprints on tiles disappear
as I watch my feet slowly dissolve,
cold working its way up my legs.
Letting go of my knees, of my thighs,
that body sat hunched on the side
as blue silence welcomes me in.

Weighing Machines

How wonderful, to revert to zero
sitting in the tiled cool
of an empty bathroom.

Or gather talcum-scented dust
among thinning sheets and towels
in the airing cupboard.

To retire from judgement,
count out our days with just
the weightless air pressing down on us.

Who wants to hover back and forth forever
between the nines and tens,
as heels are gently lifted, pressed down again,

to feel a lifetime's disappointment
at all we have to say,
defeated sighs as we are put away.

Now at night we dream in other measures:
spans and leagues and fathoms,
how in this artificial light

an undressed woman might find
her own basic equivalence instead
in bolts of silk, bushels of apples.

Miss Havisham and Lucy Jordan road
test an Alfa Romeo 4C coupe

At speeds like these   the wind lifts   cleans pea-soupers from
your hair   blows away the valium clouds   you swallow
greedy lungfuls of it   laughter unstoppered   from your
throat   astonished at the sound it makes   buffeting the
car   rattling the very frame of you   like sunlight   breaking
through   those dirty casement windows   vacuuming
cobwebbed crevices   hidden deep inside   you turn the dial
but still can't hear the radio   amid the noise   songs fizzle
to white static   unravelling like wedding veils   American
suburban homes   *we're just 37*   you shout to cars   passing
the other way   but no-one seems to notice   not that it
matters now   you've left behind   daily perambulations
through a list of chores   trails of cake crumbs   made by
dusty beetles   you've lost the map   watched it flap away
into the slipstream   beyond the clearing windscreen   years
stretch out ahead   and all road signs from here   lead
straight on to Paris

The Circus of Possibilities

To: Simpkins, Michael
From: Temp Account
Subject: The Circus of Possibilities

Apologies Mr Simpkins, I do not have the details
of this afternoon's meeting. But need to inform you
that a circus train bound for the Caucasus
leaves at 3.48. Will you run away with me?

I've watched you plot mortality assumptions
with care for weeks. But I am now convinced, Mr Simpkins,
these are not calculations for an Excel graph;
they demand to be tested on the steel of a high wire.

If I somersaulted towards you would you catch me Mr Simpkins?
I think you would. You can quantify actuarial risk
and yield curves, so I'd entrust the safety
of my rhinestoned trajectory to those measured hands.

I have informed HR. They will waive your notice period
in lieu of future pension payments.
I'm sure your wife will understand. We'll send her tickets
for the gala performance in St. Petersburg.

I have learned English, and what a fax is
so these new skills will not be difficult for you, Mr Simpkins.
Besides, this climate-controlled air conditioning
is no good at all for your constitution:

you need the bite of winter on your skin,
the struggle to peg down guy ropes in a storm.
Can you hear the steam piano? How its tune speeds up
like madness towards the end?

Log off your computer now: we'll make Sofia by dawn,
spooned on a goose-down mattress;
wake to the stink of axle grease and toffee apples,
laughing at the growl of tethered lions.

An Arsonist's Guide To Lockdown

There are tricks to keep yourself safe:
damp kitchen towels wrapped around
the matches, drawers locked, keys stashed
on your highest shelf. Make sure you bin
junk mail and newspapers, left in piles
your itching hands will want to twist
and concertina them into paper lighters.
Surround yourself with the sterile whiff
of stainless steel and iron: filing cabinets,
cutlery, heavy duty grills, the unburnable
that's dragged out blackened, warped,
yet still intact when everything you've loved
has gone. Don't think about the giddiness
as the quick flames of the kindling catch,
the warm glow from deep inside as a strut
or joist takes hold. Forget that sense of abandon,
watching a disused shed slowly collapse
in on itself. You've tried to keep yourself
in check before, but it seemed to matter less
when the world was out there to rampage in
and other people just collateral damage.
Who hasn't had relationships like that?
But now your fire-stoked demons are all curling
inwards and you're scared to breathe too hard.
Concentrate instead on the steady rain outside.

An Empty Building After Sudden Rain

This is the state I'm trying to achieve:
breath like breeze through windows.

A structural sense of things held in place,
all clutter cleared from air-filled rooms.

No trace of the person who once lived here
or thought to where they've gone.

A door open to the rain-soaked grass,
sunlight and shadow patterning the floor.

A house changes when a guest enters,
the way people do, walking through doorways

into a new room. How they suddenly
forget what they came in for, stand

in the moment, marvelling at this space,
the possibilities of blank walls.

The Dissolution Of The Libraries

Words whirled away   like thought untethering
itself.   Stand here – dugdeep in boneshells
of abandoned bookbanks – and hear
their *whisperlong* as winds blow in.

The ransacked sky-stacks   row after row
reaching to a roofdome   now rent weather-wide.
Mouldmaps inbloom   between bird-shitsplat spines;
nestled nooks   for house-spugs & mouserats.

Gone all the idolgold: the glimmerings
on paperthick and parch,   that flare, facelit,
matchbright –   magick as moonglare
suddenly uncloudclothed –   picking out a path.

Wonderwhen whole worlds were ribbed in rhyme:
scriptsafe, bookbound.   A hoard of heartsong.
Secrets storied like spels   to ken, to keen,
to kindl   warmfire in winterdarks.

O weary word-wanderers   travelsore and tired
hopesmirched so homefar home.   Timesgone
when sounds ink-sketched slipt moutheasy
into meaning. Didn't fur tongue   taste foreignfull.

Booksmell

Boxing up books for Oxfam I am struck
by it: the wood-soaked tang as I flick through
my Penguin Modern Classics. Worlds I knew
caught in the earthy base notes of an Iris Murdoch.
Can they be that old? These tatty paperbacks
I inhaled throughout my teens and twenties,
familiar covers coffee-ringed in places,
blue spines bent, piled up in tottering stacks.

Not quite the damp maltiness of a gold
edged leather-bound Tennyson or Dickens.
But all their pages ooze the same nostalgic
chemicals of cosy afternoons moulded
to a sofa. That slow burn of humdrum magic,
like hour hands you don't see quickening.

A Pindaric Ode to Robert Smith of The Cure

The gods do not change. Apollo remains
resolutely Apollo. So half obscured and through
a haze of dry ice and strobing spotlights,
you emerge, stage left; backcombed hair ablaze.

We are not sixteen. Those girls bold
with mascara and magic marker eyeliner
have transformed themselves into shapes
we least expected, and sometimes barely recognise.

But still, the opening riff of *Charlotte Sometimes*
lifts us through the hairspray fog
back to single bedrooms, wonky posters peeling
from the ceiling, and all that wasted heartache.

O Robert Smith, tower above the lesser deities
we idolised: the cowboy-booted tax-swervers
and self-obsessed who now are all *Viva Hate*.
(Yes, Morrissey and Bono, I'm looking straight at you.)

You stride colossus-like from past to present:
guitar slung low, a wry belipsticked smile.
Tonight belongs to ageing goths and scrawly love songs.
Nothing has altered. It all remains the same.

Wonderstuff

The label says this blue whale's heart, (the largest thing to love I guess) is the size of a cow, that song we used to dance to back in 1991, when being young seemed ordinary. Dear Jules, who sent love letters in cornflakes packets (postage based on weight not size back then), I thought of you today in the museum, looking at this heart pulled from its element: it took four marine biologists to haul it through the ribs you know. It says here there are whales alive today who were swimming in Arctic seas before Melville picked up his pen (hard to believe I know). A blue whale's heart beats slowly – twice a minute – the average lifespan of whales or shrews or wallabies is constant, when measured out in heartbeats, not by years (or spoons). Anyway if you are reading this it could be decades from now, and all these whales have gone, and there are just museums trying to explain in easy-to-imagine terms the vastness of what's been lost. Your heart was on a plinth like this, so visible, so shocking.

The heart is not a ♥ and not the heart of you

I'd rather have a pig's heart. They seem robust
emotionally. Always rootling for good stuff.
And loyal. At school I weighed one in my palm.
It felt strong enough. Firm and muscly.
And when I pushed in the glass tube to inflate
a ventricle the mechanics all worked perfectly
despite its butchered state. Not scarred. Not broken.
One dark clot oozing from the pulmonary vein
like a single teardrop, waiting to be dabbed away,
before the pig gets on again with all its piggy things.
The kind of heart those girls squealing on the bench
behind would like. A pig's heart is valentine-shaped,
sits dead centre in its chest, beating wildly.
Not this off kilter ache which still unbalances me.

Darling, you look like £739,905 in that dress

according to today's Valentine exchange rate
on Google. Please press your fingers, lightly,
to my neck, see how my tacky pulse will quicken.
The sparkles in our eyes, you know, are nothing
more than postponed tears, or stifled yawns,
perhaps from reading all those moonsick poets.
I want to say it with potato plants, for benevolence
and misplaced optimism. Look how their shoots
resemble alien spider legs entwining each other,
while they slowly suffocate in plastic bags
at the back of our dark cupboards. Falling in love
on a suspension bridge is just an old experiment
proving romance isn't dead, it's only the dizziness
and fear you sometimes get close to the edge,
staring down into ravines of nothingness.

Bad Feminists
With only a few apologies to Robert Browning

Here's David Beckham, looking as if he were alive.
The breathing slow and metrical, that steady rise
and fall of his stupendous chest. Caught on film,
spooled day and night inside this darkened room
for us selected few – the women who appreciate
a perfect nude, swathed in Egyptian cotton sheets.
Though quite untouchable. Still, it works both ways.
He will not raise a hand nor undermine a word you say,
open an eye to find your body wanting –
he'll just sleep on, indefinitely, the gothic font
of each tattoo rippling in the light like animated ink.
An artwork on an artwork, or so I like to think.
These days who doesn't want to play post-gender
post-identity games. Some call the piece a wonder
now: no thrusting David lording it from his pedestal,
but here in bed, supine, surrendered, vulnerable.
You noticed, no doubt – smart women always do –
my use of the conditional subjunctive. It's true,
his whereabouts are not now known. Sam Taylor-Wood
could have explained, but why should an artist stoop
to deny claims that suspected murder was a ruse
to inflate a portrait's worth? As you know, she chooses
never to stoop. It soon became a viral trend: so many men
caught sleeping. Their dreamy half-smiles frozen
for all eternity – a crying shame so few smiled half
as charmingly when wide awake. The photographs
and phone footage quickly multiplied. It was claimed
some disappeared, leaving just these silent bodies framed,
seemingly alive, yet not alive. Some have objected

to galleries displaying these 'spots of joy' I have collected.
Such trifling complaints! from those quick to find fault or blame,
their passions, like their anger, all too easily inflamed,
peeved that a comic slant on the male form informs our view.
Well-read critics – which I am not – say none of this is new.
At least their names remain. Titles that have tumbled down
the centuries, appended now to *objets d'art* – and owned.
Projected onto pink-washed walls, pleasing backdrops
for soirées hosted by bad feminists like me. A step up
from *chichi* dinner parties served on Judy Chicago plates.
It's almost time to leave. Cocktails will be served at eight.
But as we head downstairs, listen out for *Artemis*,
our new sound installation, fresh from the Venice
Biennale. You can just detect the baying hounds
beneath the unchecked roar of laughter echoing around.

Still Life: Ironing Pile as White Rhino

It emits a disgruntled air
as I keep a respectful distance
pretending to ignore it.

A rugged look of something
monumental
used to just standing there

dreaming of acacia leaves,
creases worn so deep
they concertina up like worry lines.

Of course white rhinos
are only white when a full moon
washes the savannah.

On days like this they glower
dust-baked grey, shades
of school vests and stretched elastic.

And black rhinos
are not black at all. They lurk
in airing cupboards

bleached out, faded, over-wrung,
proving the rule:
all things converge to grey.

Casting a wary glance
I take a slow step or two
further back

from this brooding hulk
of household chores.
Although sometimes I dream

the hot hoof of an iron,
want its snorting steam
to smooth the tired folds

in heavy legs, ease out the ache
of all those lonely sleeves,
before it is too late.

Nest of Scarves

They're still there
twisted round each other
like floral-printed snakes.
Purple silk ones, tasselled reds
in some rich material
I want to call damask,
workday blues and greens
from Next and M&S.
One Christmas I fashioned one
into a shepherd's headdress
and when I opened up the bag
the perfumed scent
was like her voice
speaking in tongues.
It shocked me back years.
Afterwards I folded up
the plastic carefully
to stop what particles
remained drifting,
being lost in the stale air
of shoes and handbags
on my wardrobe floor.
I eye the closed bag
from time to time
too scared to open it
and breathe the last scent,
or find the last scent gone.
The scarves knot inside
the scent of a memory
with the memory of a scent.

Visiting the Dead

Mum says not ram's blood tonight dear
so I pour a glass of Merlot.

It's been 10 years wandering
but for now we just swirl silence.

She moves closer to the fire, asks how
I found her here – and for a moment

I am lost in those elaborate directions,
the path of stars you navigate through sorrow.

Once you stop looking, there are more doors
than you'd think leading to the underworld:

a downstairs bookshop with its rows
of second-hand detective novels,

the kitchen tiles that double as a trapdoor
when certain songs play on the radio,

the way my hand holds a glass of whisky.
The shades crowd in, and here's my friend

who left too recently, too soon.
The suddenness of death, it winds you

with the weight of unspent afternoons.
Absence is a debt we can't repay,

but it creates small gaps, a chink where light
or love, or what is left, leaks round closed doors,

illuminating them, showing where to push
to let the things you've lost step through.

Floating Islands

I conjure up their would-be perfect peaks:
  puffball meringues, lacy as Botticelli clouds
    almost levitating
like a dream across the unrippled surface
    of a cream-thin custard.

A Day-Glo picture from the recipe cards
  mum filed away in a yellow plastic box.
    Remember times
we teased her for sunken realities
    the stodgy egginess

that soon became the end-point on a scale
  of the overcooked, unrisen, seared,
    stuck-in-the-tin.
At least it's not a floating island
    dad used to say.

But now they cast long shadows over me
  as kids fork through reheated bolognese
    for rogue onions,
pull faces, push their plates away,
    demand McDonalds.

They rise up through the haze, magnificent,
  with all their Tuesday night ambition,
    visions in white
spun from the spoon-soft give of memories,
    sugar-coated mountains.

White Blancmange Rabbit

A neighbour brought it round
the day after grandma died.
It sat, ears back, on a green plate
faintly quivering

the way a rabbit might
among the grass, crouched low
waiting for the shadow of a cat
or fox to pass.

A kindness of sugar, set milk
and glossy arrowroot. My sister
spooned a mouthful from its flank,
and retched.

After a week where it sat
in the fridge, slowly yellowing.
After the funeral, when it was
slid into the bin

with the uneaten sandwiches
and casseroles. After the plate
was cleaned so you could see
its fancy edging.

After Margaret called round
I watched mum thank her,
saying how much the girls
enjoyed it,

as though, after all this, she was free
to say anything, anything at all,
was making it up from here
with no-one watching.

Plait

The trick is to hold three braids in two hands
and ignore the logistics of mornings.
Wind the first over the second, then cross

the third over the first, and so on. Don't get cross
as arguments slip like hoarded minutes out of hand.
Flex zen-calmed fingers: remember even school mornings

don't last forever. Focus on this Tuesday morning,
soft nape and collar crease, the wonky plait. Let its criss cross
weave its ordinary magic, like a proverb handed

across the generations, mourning there is never enough time,
                                        but just enough hands.

Love Makes Your Scalp Itch

I know because I've combed / week after week / each strand of
their lovely heads / unloosened pony tails / tugged and pulled
/ from root to tip / to clean unplaited hanks / of crawling lice
/ their unhatched eggs / the weapon of my choice / a metal
close-toothed comb / that digs and scratches / I've watched
a louse / belly fat with blood / climb up a golden thread /
snapped its back / with my thumbnail / in a satisfying crack
/ my daughters wrapped in towels / one sitting on the bath /
chemical shampoo / dripping down her neck / the other knelt
in front of me / fidgeting and crying / wanting to go to bed /
this is love's grittiness / compelling you / month after month /
to do what must be done / like the cycle of a fairy-tale / those
lovely heads / tipped from side to side / to catch the light / as
though I'm pouring stories in their ears / the louse that laid a
hundred golden eggs / the girls whose tangled hair betrayed
them / the mother who raked pins through their scalp / a
close-toothed comb that kept its secrets / the never-endingness
of it / the need to scratch an itch / a story starting up again

For The Bear Spotters

It's in our blood. Our genes.
That homeopathic trace of long dead ancestors.

The way talk flows as easily as a second bottle
opened on a school night. How you huddle

close to friends, freezing in spangly tops,
counting down the hour to the night bus.

No lark full mornings fat with worms for us.
The sunrises we see are heading home,

or bleeding like a headache through a skylight
as sleep at last strong-arms insomnia.

We're the ones who stretch the day beyond
its moon-edged limits. Steal dreaming hours,

fill them with other wild-eyed stuff. The dancing queens
and ballad spinners, the lock-in karaoke singers,

midnight guitar noodlers looping a soft refrain,
the one-more-for-the-roaders with their one last tale.

We are the candle burners, flame watchers, fire stokers,
listening for footsteps in the dark,

the middle-distance gazers, deciphering the shadows
to see which hold teeth and fur.

Lady Macbeth Jam

He who wants plums plants for his sons
He who wants damsons plants for his grandsons
Trad.

Well, that's what we called it,
that summer of wasps and the tree
now bearing down with them.
Bowl after bowl of damsons.
The devil's plum. It refuses
to give up its stone heart easily,
clings to bitter flesh.
Grandma hands me a knife
from the drawer of sharp things
we're not allowed into.
Our fingers purpling, as we slice
and twist and dig, red wetness
seeping through a cloth underneath.
The pan on the hob at a slow simmer,
as she stirs figures of eight
through the bubbling mess,
clockwise to sugar tartness,
anti-clockwise to set.
Jars on the sill stood wide-mouthed,
waiting. I press waxed discs
to curdling skin, feel stickiness
like a wound healing,
close eyes with each lid.
Scrub stained fingers raw with lemon juice.
There's not a colour like it
on the pantry shelf. You could melt

a crown of black prince rubies,
net shepherds' sunsets
through cathedral windows
and still not own the darkness
of this swirl. We spread
the sweetness thick on toast.
Spit out splinters of missed stones.

Grandma Frankenstein

She bottles goosegogs,
topped and tailed,
yellowed orbs
that stare like bulls' eyes
from the loggia shelf.

Chubby rhubarb logs
embalmed in jars,
syrup-steeped
to leach away
tongue-tart pinkness.

Rows of broad beans,
cabbage hearts and marrow.
Runners sliced along
the diagonal,
tenderised in salt.

Sealed harvest light
in jams and chutneys.
Windfalls bagged,
waiting for crunch
to slump to mush.

She spoons the gloop
into a Sunday pie dish.
Grey-green matter
galvanised with a lick
of winter gravy.

Grandma Frankenstein's Needle Book

It prickles with old magic. The kind used to bind
castles in thorn thickets when years fell silent.

A glitter of needles. Points sharp as frosted stars,
trailing their loose threads across each felted page.

All those faded blues and yellows, an unravelling
of picnic rugs and petticoats, the last tie

to lost buttons. And there's grandma sitting
in the armchair by the fire, gathering night

about her in thick pleats, patching torn knees.
Mouth full of pins, as she warns my sister

her lips will be sewn shut if she says that again.
I step up onto the stool so she can lower hems,

let out darts on dresses that pinch under arms,
pull across my chest. A girl who can't stop growing.

We watch her frogging princess seams,
laying out a different paper pattern in its place.

She teaches us slip stitches, to work the wrong
side of the cloth, tuck messy ends away.

How to mend. You just need the right tools.
There are needles for everything, lace and linen,

leather, skin. She shows us how to quilt
a coat from offcuts, lose ourselves inside

embroidered details. Sometimes she complains
about poor light, borrows our eyes again,

says she needs their cat-like quickness,
those flecks of green that she had once.

One swift lick of thumb and forefinger
to smooth cotton ends, twirl them to a point,

guide thread through the black hole
at the centre of the needle, staring back at me.

Foraging for Grandma Frankenstein

Sometimes I pretend the slug tracks
are simply lip gloss on the grass.
I follow them, to where the nettles
clump, and snip some for my bag.
She's given me her list: feverfew,
dandelions, wild garlic. Best picked
at dawn, when they are full of scent
and sap, before sun pokes through
the damp underbelly of hedgerows.
Grandma says I fuss too much,
about the spider webs that brush
my face, catch in my hair. But says
I must whisper a quick prayer
for snails crushed beneath my sandals.
She won't listen to my arguments,
says she's too old for stooping now,
her knees don't like the dew.
Besides things picked by girls' fingers
hold their magic, the softness of our skin
won't bruise tender stems, mash berries.
Today, it's four thieves vinegar
she's brewing. I dig fingers into mud
to ease out roots, watch worms squirm
away, light rippling their meaty skin,
telling them to burrow deeper, disappear
through dirt. Sometimes out here alone
I'll rub cuckoo spit into the leaves,
tie up my haul with curses, hoping
it will spoil her soups and poultices,
so cramps will worsen, colicky babies

will still scream the night away,
and no more neighbours will come calling.
But then I feel a needling up my arms,
like the burn of gritty stars, and know
with all the certainty of earthworms,
she's watching through the frosted air.

The Great Aunts

Every summer there'd be an afternoon
of visiting, sitting in front rooms
where windows rarely opened,
being asked to stand up straight
to see how much we'd grown.
Warned not to touch the Scottie dog
or china ballerinas dancing
between the various knick-knacks
on their crowded mantle-shelves.
They'd fan pink wafers, jaffa cakes
and wagon wheels on paper doilies,
pretend not to hear mum saying
that's enough now to offer us another.
When it was time to go, they'd rummage
in handbags smelling of butterscotch
for pocket money, kisses on our cheeks
damp as lemon sponge. Sometimes Dad
would drive them to Shorehead for tea,
where they'd pick at fish and chips,
before devouring ice-cream sundaes
topped with glacé cherries, rainbow sprinkles.
The talk of poor Harry, Andrew, Dave –
even now I'm not sure who was married
to whose brother, which ones were simply
nana's friends. These bird-like women,
hips held in place by pins, who just craved
a little sugar at the end, their desserts
in fancy glasses, eaten with long spoons.

Swallows Rest Home

How frail they look, in lonely rows
perched in wing-back chairs, staring
as sky rolls through day-room windows.

Tucked away within themselves, they sit
for hours. Watch carers fuss with cups of tea,
pick crumbs from plates in front of them.

They've lost their grip on telephone wires,
flown into cloud; it fogs the stars
makes it hard to find their bearings.

Beneath the TCP and talcum powder
a tang of aviaries, clipped wings.
They're bruised from falls, pipe bones

now shattered, pinned back in place.
Nested in pillows, earthbound, bedsore.
Some days a reed-thin song catches the air

swoops and soars above their heads.
Behind closed eyes they dream the miles
slipping away beneath as they take flight.

The Visitors

That morning we lost count. You said perhaps
  a thousand geese hauling in a cold front from the coast.
Skein after skein of them, skimming roofs so low

we could feel the wind shift with each beat
  of wing, a drum to their honked warnings. Overhead
they raked the sky into straggly chevrons

like loose ends of wool untucked, or thought
  pulled through the clouds of a hard year. The air was charged
with them, alive and strange in these spare days

before New Year. We were just visitors
  and couldn't say if their arrival or passing were commonplace,
or some rare slot of moon and weather.

Looking up, you said it's easy to be wonderstruck
  by numbers in a flock, the miles they fly, the way grey
silvers in low winter light, brightens the sky.

We fashion our own omens. Some sign
  perhaps, or nothing more than songs of snow
from Latvia, tilt of northern hemispheres.

On Easter Sunday I Awoke

to birdsong in the dark.
The pigeons carousing from lamp posts,
while a riot of blue-tits and finches,
dunnocks and robins tried to drown out the jays
and woodcocks and warblers from Epping Forest.

And I swore as the sun edged round the blinds,
further back, I could pick out pelicans, peacocks,
ospreys, oyster-catchers, hornbills, hoopoes
and cockatoos, singing so loud that for a moment
I could barely hear the traffic, relentless even now,
on the North Circular. And I'd been dreaming

that a man stood before me with a knife,
its blade red and wet. I tried to hold
my hands up, cross the street and back away,
but you know how it is in dreams,
how your heels catch and pavements roll on forever.

It sounds as if I must have made it up: waking up
to all this. Does it matter today that the churches
are full of empty air, rose windows casting unseen
kaleidoscopes of sunlight on the floor? So much
pours in through a skylight regardless,
though it seems no consolation at the time.

Walking on Water, Beginners Class

Expect to get wet.[1] The sudden plunge[2]
    from higher consciousness
        into the cold[3] and chlorinated dark

is what we call our Monday morning
    mind-spritz,[4] while the urge to kick upwards
        will work wonders for the glutes.

Welcome to the deep end: a six week
    immersive workout[5] for those who've paddled
        through the shallow widths of faith.[6]

Step by step we'll test the surface tension
    in our lives, pivot legs, refocus core,
        perfect our pondskater positions[7]

by distributing weight as far as possible
    (which, I appreciate, can be more difficult
        for some than others).

---

1   Course unsuitable for non-swimmers and/or agnostically-inclined
2   Always step into the unknown. No diving. Max depth 1.2m
3   Pool temperature maintained at 28.4°C
4   Please note there is no Walking on Water on bank holidays
5   Deposit required to secure place. No refunds for missed sessions
6   Details of 'Shallow Widths of Faith' course on website. Floats provided
7   See also Jesus Bug pose (US Eng.) or epipleustonicasana (New Aquarian babblespeak)

By the balm of cool water[8] on your soles[9]
you'll master the meniscus, have no fear
of flux, learn to love a blue edge.[10]

Some stride. Others duck and bob-up
spitting out a flawless Möbius loop.[11]
Miracles work their own ways.[12]

Notice the way your feet ripple the light.
And don't forget when walking out[13] to pause –
and give way to those swimming lengths.[14]

8   See point 3 for clarification
9   No outdoor footwear poolside. Plastic shoes (sliders/ crocs/ flip-
    flops) not recommended for water-walking activities
10 We define the concept of walking on water in accordance with
    what oneself believes or senses, see Daniel von Wachter, *Concepts
    of Miracle* (International Academy of Philosophy, Liechtenstein) for
    further clarification
11 Spitting of non-Möbius loops strictly prohibited
12 No external certification of miracles provided, cf David Hume
    in *Of Miracles* (Section X. of *An Enquiry Concerning Human
    Understanding*)
13 No running
14 Classes run concurrently with lane swimming (adult fitness)
    10–11.30 a.m.

Soulscabber

Lord, lead us not into temptation.
Those girls with unchewed plaits resist
the itchiness, this feel of knitting flesh,
but the devil loves a bitten fingernail.
Mine work away across the scabby crust,
its cratered surface cheesy as the moon
drying from sticky green to yellow to dark red.
I dig in at one side, lift up a tender edge –
too soon, too soon. It weeps a little pus.
This sting of liquid skin, bubbling beneath
all hot and restless. I try to close the lid
back on my knee. But it won't fit.
A secret sort of hurt that makes me want
to pick and pick away at it. I score a crease,
fold a corner back, unthread the leg hairs
holding it in place. And slowly prise bits off.
A not-so-perfect disc, utterly unsoullike.
I shouldn't prod at wounds, but learn to wait
until they're paper-thin and wafery.
Not this chewy mess, fizzing on my tongue.

Mouthfeel

Michelin-starred chefs do it blindfold,
apparently, in the afternoon lull after lunch service.

Raw liver on the tongue, peeled muscat grapes,
forkful of sea-bream with bones. It's not the taste,

they want to know the feel of it first hand,
hold it there, roll it around. You have to relish it all:

clumsy wetness of a teenage kiss, teeth knocking,
to those barely brushing lips, a silkweave graze

you sometimes still crave. Now when our mouths
meet the grooves of one another they take

what sustenance they need. No fuss, or fanciness.
We let words come. You might say *archipelago,*

I'll try *flimflam* or *scuttlebutt*. And we'll laugh
on cleanly-laundered sheets, deliciously.

The Flesh Delusion

Look at them, sitting on deckchairs
    strolling the lawns
convinced they're solid, corpulent.

Unbreakable, each movement seems to say.
      The careless arms
  heads tipped precariously   with each guffaw.

     Such confidence in built realities.
           They do not seem to see
  windows   opening up inside them.

How strange it seems to us
          not to anticipate
    a shattering;

not to dream the twisted intricacies
    of Murano chandeliers,
        glass pianos, crystalware;

  not to wake each day
      with nerves   a feedback loop
of champagne flutes   slipping from our fingers.

    Not to see yourself refracted
through cracked panes
    in pavilioned greenhouses   and mirror mazes.

Perhaps they don't fear love at all.
                    Or crave its touch.
          Can't grasp its resonant frequencies:

          how when it hits the high notes
you will disintegrate
                              into a thousand star-like pieces.

Souvenirs

Today is not the day you're going to die. You watch a cat
stalk the shadow of a fly across the garage roof.
Today is not the day you're going to die.

Others might. But they are not your others. Not today.
Workmen digging holes outside contemplate
the mess of wires below. The trees remain

astonishingly plain, untroubled by blossom
or a weight of leaves on the turn. Nothing significant
outside, just cats and flies and workmen,

temporarily elevated because today
– and almost every day beyond – are days
where you don't die. Seizing each one is exhausting.

It's ok if some stand ordinary: a desk, a book, a view.
You think these days are like the plates
your mother mounted on her kitchen wall, small souvenirs:

'Greetings from Bruges', or a blackbird against
an orange check design, the gilt around a latticed edge
caught by the under-cupboard lights,

framing a fragile whiteness. And on days like this
you are once more taken aback how they hold
the very idea of breaking, but still remain intact.

Indoor Cloudspotting

Yesterday was leadbellied. Bearing down not floating away. A
sense of nimbostratus gathering shadows outside the kitchen
windows. You tick the box marked 'chance of rain'. We're
classifying drift, tabulating it into neat rows. Deciding on
the exact amount of wisp needed to separate cirrus from
cirro-cumulus, mark out the edges of another Tuesday.
Constable had it right. Those paintings where the sky's the
only thing alive and moving. Our eyes are drawn to it. Away
from dull foregrounds where doors are painted shut. Bodies
without surface, someone said. Carrying cathedrals of rain.
Sometimes the sun cuts sieve-like holes through us and we
can't hold it any longer, cry stair rods for hours. We've made
a colour wheel that turns through dolomite and mole to
unironed pillowcase, the empty page. Argue into dusk where
one shade of loneliness leaches into another. You disagree.
Or perhaps I do. It's hard to tell through perpetual mizzle
of low-lying stratus. Sometimes it's just my own unbodied
surface in the darkening glass. This morning is more weasel-
backed you say. Though shapes are ill-defined. They lack
a Latin taxonomy to orient ourselves around. We're losing
count of all our airy citadels, these dragonish days.

Sunrise with Sea Monsters
after JMW Turner

In the morning light they fade
a little. Impressions of tentacles and teeth
you know could drag you under.

Today will be a good day. Look
how a hazy sun bleeds into everything,
burns off the swirling sea haar,

touches the darkness of the water
with just a hint of fire.
Keep a steady gaze on fixed horizons.

The old leviathan is sleeping now.
Try not to think about iron ships
bellowing steam, a winch of chains,

mouth cranked wide, ready to swallow
all colour up into its black insides.
The sky, for now, still holds.

Don't stare too closely at the clouds.
Too many monsters there, all ill-defined.
Too few sunrises left to face them down.

Organised Water

the mind is its own jellyfish
propelling itself   somewhat waywardly

through its own element
thinking thoughts   about thought

a miracle really   how it holds
an impression of form

does not dissolve   lose all sense
of its aqueous self to the vastness

of oceans   but still flows
into the scoop of a net or a bucket

pourable   yet distinct
caught up some nights

in the light   of its own
luminescent ideas

Acknowledgements

Thanks to the editors of the magazines and online journals *14 Magazine*, *Under the Radar*, *The Rialto*, *The North*, *Spelt Magazine*, *The High Window*, *The Friday Poem*, *Finished Creatures*, *Atrium*, *Three Drops from a Cauldron* and *Write Where We Are Now (MMU)* where some of these poems first appeared.

'Dear Bees –' was the winner of the Live Canon International Poetry Competition (2021); 'Love Makes Your Scalp Itch' was the winner of the YorkMix Poetry Prize (2021), where 'Quantum Theory of Moss' was also highly commended; 'Mushrooms' was the winner of Ver Poets Competition (2018); 'Plait' was the winner in the Prole Laureate Competition (2013); 'My Life as a B-list Movie Star' was placed fourth in the Kent and Sussex Poetry Society Competition (2023), 'Floating Islands' was commended in the Ware Poets Prize (2022); 'The Visitors' was a runner up in the Keats-Shelley Poetry Prize (2020) and 'Wonderstuff' was long listed for the National Poetry Competition (2020).

Thank you to the editors of both the Emma Press and Smith|Doorstop: a handful of these poems first appeared in pamphlets published with these excellent presses. I'm also grateful for the support of the Jerwood Arvon Mentoring scheme.

These poems have not been written in splendid isolation, but have been inspired and shaped by the good company and wise words of fellow poets in workshops and courses in recent years. Particular thanks to Caroline Bird, Tamar Yoseloff and

Glyn Maxwell, Peter and Ann Sansom, Jacqueline Saphra, Jonathan Edwards, Miriam Nash and Wendy Pratt for being such inspiring and encouraging teachers. Thanks also to those who generously read and re-read early manuscript copies, particularly Kathy Pimlott, Ramona Herdman, Ken Evans and Anne Symons. And special thanks to Sara Levy — for her excellent proofing skills and fine company.

Many thanks to Chris Hamilton-Emery and Salt Publishing for making a home for this collection and designing such an eye-catching cover. I will be happy to be judged by it.

And finally, but most importantly, thanks to Steve, Susie and Kitt for their love and support, and giving me the time to write.

This book has been typeset by
SALT PUBLISHING LIMITED
using Sabon, a font designed by Jan Tschichold
for the D. Stempel AG, Linotype and Monotype Foundries.
It is manufactured using Holmen Book Cream 70gsm,
a Forest Stewardship Council™ certified paper from the
Hallsta Paper Mill in Sweden. It was printed and bound
by Clays Limited in Bungay, Suffolk, Great Britain.

SHEFFIELD
GREAT BRITAIN
MMXXIII